Skelectal Family's Skeletons of Eternity

by

Otis Bennett, Jr.

ISBN: 0-75965-581-2

This book is printed on acid free paper.

1stBooks - rev. 07/24/01

Fresh

Issues and issues and
issues...
that slide...
into the void of eternities...
one
love...
beautifies me, it is a
deifying
of
godliness...
of
me,
jackls of the night,
in fuse...
in...
perplexed
modes
of
question...

Otis Bennett, Jr.

of
death-machinery
that
justly…is
not
there.

The sychronicity...
playing...
the
game...
of
judgement,
knows
the
desperation
of
absurdity
and
falseness,

Otis Bennett, Jr.

so
winners
are...
the
New...
Breed...

Soda-sweet-
candy-bar-
greetings
cause
materialization
of
new-
breed-
introductions
to
motion,
that
consumes

day
and
night...

So
the
intent
of
the
sillohuette-motion
breaks
through,
to
the
other-side,
a
rejoicer...
of
the
new

vastness,
no
longer
crushing
their
arms...
with...
knives...
attached
to
hammers...

Night: Thursday March 8, 2001

Inward...
vats of
thought...night-aire...
a...
motion
that
stands still,
molecular-
high-of-
silence...
burning...
warps
through
time,
to
a
time

hoped
for...

There is...
no
right
now...
only
silence ________,
of
the
wandering-of-the-
mind...
I
mind-
my-
own-
business...
and
yet

still...
still...
as
I...
might...
be...
there's
the
tropical
tree.

In
other
words...
the...
flight...
was
canceled...

Otis Bennett, Jr.

This Lord Prayer

To...
score...
the
impossible...
act...__________,
to...
vanish...
as
a
man...of
uneasy
feelings
of
a
fire gallery...this...
sets
these
meditations
into...

odds...
chance...
probability
of
a
sanctuary...
seen...
in...
the
fire-gallery's
far off,
hazy
smoke...
my
wonderment,
breathes
the
nectar
of

puzzlement...
this
is...
quite
possibly...
a...
being's
attempt...
at...
intense...
meditation...
reflection...

To
absorb...
tin-
metallic-
swooms
of
aeresol...

a
look
into
the
eyes
of
a
manchyle...me...myself
in
a
bathroom...
mirror...
hazily...
feebly...
almost
unconscious...__________,
yet...________,
thanking
God

that...
it
wasn't
my
time...
angrily...
sadly...
in
my
time...

All
of
this...
for
her...
name...
wait...

Otis Bennett, Jr.

no,
all
of
this
for
that...
that...
that
eludes...
definity...__________,
in
reason...
and
meaning...
for
dope-rainy-wet-
days
with
unrest...
a...

worldly,
communicating
word
of
monster...
living
God
or
dead
God...
Chapter: I don’t know...
Verse: I don’t know...

IN WHY RESIDENT

I...
am……
a...
citizen
of
the United States...
I...
am...
not
a...citizen
of...
the...
United...
States...
I
from...
a...
death-wound...
cried...I...
beared

my...
heart...in
heat...
bloodshed
and
bullets...as all
saw...as...years
passed...before...a...realizing
said...
it...
was...__________,
to...
be...either or for the masses,
out of meek ness,
out of despair
out of disgust...
out of dissatisfaction...
I
beared
a...

heart...
bleeding...
the
songs
of
the
power
of
any...who are...
denied...
precious...precious...
precious...
choice...

Death: Ting Tu Whan Khay

A...
sight
as...
a
image
mirrored...
a...
reflection
of
the
ghost...an abandoned
Tenament
possessed
of
both
owner...
and
dweller...
beyond

description...
it
howls
at
the
warmth
of
the
west...
possibly...__________,
a
way...
out...
for
the
flowing
Sabbath
of...
martyrs
for...__________,

a
new
sphere...
long-
over-
due...
in
the
heavens
of
Earth...

Silent
murmurs...
distant...the
weak...
retribution
for
summer
to

autumn...
release
me,
release
me,
release
me...
I...
am
no
longer
primitive...I
released
from
this
rhetoric...
resides
within
the
light-

years
that
breathe
eternals
breathe...

Sipping
on...
eternity's
life...
I...
a
cripple
of
U. S. A's
disciplinary
measure
must...
show...

it
how
to
discipline...
gently

An
announcement
from
the
circle
sphere
of
those
who
have
forfeited
must
not

fall
to
ears
that
have
been
condemned,
by
the
dust
of
being
deadened...

Sound...enlivens
one love...
one love...
one world...
nation...

American Child

Oh...mist of...the
distance...oh...mist
a desolation...__________,
the___________,
hereditary...truth...
that...
ebbs...from...your
familiarity...
with
the
sillhouette...deep...
with
no
destination...
oh
mist...the
unfinished
dialectec
mimic

Otis Bennett, Jr.

rings
oer'
the
infinite...

Toll...
of
drama...that
ends
with
many...reenacting...
struggling...
to...__________,
reinforce...the...he
that...just...
has
been
destroyed...the...steno
of
their

drenching
sweat...them...
groping...
is
a
crucifixon
and
reaffirmation
that
I...once...too
lived...
insanely...
escaping...from...
nothing...

Oh mist...
great
is...
the
plumet

of
a
bird
born...
deformed...no
wings...a victim
judgement and
sentence
malicious...for
there...
are...many...predatory
...hungry...
of
no
mercy...
unfortunately
envious
of that...
which is perceived...as
that which can fly.

Otis Bennett, Jr.

The House that Jack Built

There was a...
definite...empty
dryness
on
the...striving
...the...search
for...
a
place
where
those
not
over-enchanted...
could...
define
a
new...
day__________,

the
rising
sun...the
rising...
from...
the...ash
of
a
divided
yesterday...

Color...
of
answers...was
deified...blue...a...
conjugation
of
rhythm...and blues
...

drunkardness...the
forseen...envisioned
with
much...avoidance
the
longest
day
that
the
fried-fish-carry-out-
never-understood
believers
like...me...__________,
and...those
in
Sabbatical...
prayer
like
me
would...

have...to...
cosmetically
readjust
to...
that
came
like
ghost-like...
flying
phalluses...

Someone...no...
many...
ghost-like, deep...airy
eerie,
cold
passage ways...to
the next
lyfe

expounded...
my
conversationalist
pre empting...of
love...of sex...as...
a...
result...I...will
never...
know...who
I...
am...
but...
I...
hold...a
truth...to...
be
self-evident...for...
all
for...
us...

sharing
bread...
and
water...
only...
amongst...
ourselves
and
our
babies
that
there...
is
no
regret...so...often
for...
so...
much...
lost...

Only Love

The...
meadow...all...aglow...
metamorphosis...
of
wonderment...for a moment
love...
is
two
gods...making...love
...the night...
today...as...it
is...
shall...be_________,
for
them
pure...
the...illumination

Otis Bennett, Jr.

of...the...
image...
that
is
only...
two
gods...
lovers?

Wine...a terrible...
cost...of
seperation...
lovers?

Natakini Serenade...
something
to
make
syrup-sweet-

and
in
the
enactment
of
consummation
the
play-scene
in
this
I vague,
hazy,
sight
is
judged
to
be
good...

4
the
balance...
in
her
hands__________,
justice
dances

Believable...
are
the
night's
breed..._________,
I
am
a
night-child...
a
resurrected

fact...
of
childish
wonderment
watching
telepathically
the
ocean's
rushing
meet
the
shore...
love!

Christ: To Communicate an Image

The fantasy...
of...
an
eternity...
the
fantasy...of
never...
the
blind...eye...
then
the...seeing
eye...that
marvels
at
the
sacrifices
that...
are...
the...
costs

of...
survival...deaf
ears
that
don't
hear...
a
belonging...
of...
a
longing...
that
is
a
repentance__________,
swearing...
to
God
for

mercy
mercy
mercy__________,
sweet-
loving-
chile-of mercy...
in
whatever...
form...
cries
cries
cries...
for...
mercy...

Two Left Shoes

I
acknowledge...
the
maker...the...
maker
of
all
things...then
I...
spit...
out
at
myself...
two...
left
shoes...
I
have...
no...

rite...
spring
effodes
the
swaddling
birth
of...
Jym...
Morrison...
sea...
the
sons
of
God
have
spoken...
wild...
we...
continue

Otis Bennett, Jr.

two...
dream
in
metaphors...
beyond
the
galaxies...
witch
we
must...
return
to...
sea...

NOTES

NOTES

NOTES

NOTES

NOTES

NOTES

NOTES

NOTES

NOTES

NOTES

NOTES

NOTES

NOTES

About the Author

I believe in a oneness.... A nirvana that is shared in the silent flame of the heartbeat of life. However, it has to be silent, in times, when all sharing, it should be as loud as God's trombones.... Man and woman and child have a gift of sight.... Yet consciousness can be blind, out of fear, out of opposition... out of death.... Day is night... night is day.... But the ever-flowing fountain of life is a constant heartbeat... voice... then too... silence... a harmony of our God.

www.ingramcontent.com/pod-product-compliance
Ingram Content Group UK Ltd.
Pitfield, Milton Keynes, MK11 3LW, UK
UKHW041821200726
13854UKWH00001BA/259